Riddles of Abagusii of Kenya

Gems of Wisdom from the African Continent

Christopher Okemwa

Copyright © 2011 Christopher Okemwa
All rights reserved.

This publication may not be reproduced, in whole or in part, by any means including photocopying or any information storage or retrieval system, without the specific and prior written permission of the author and publisher.

This book is sold subject to the condition that it shall not, by way of trade or otherwise, be re-sold, hired out, or otherwise circulated without the author's or publisher's prior consent in any form of binding or cover other than that in which it is published and without a similar condition including this condition being imposed on the subsequent purchaser.

First Edition: December 2011
Published by Nsemia Inc. Publishers (www.nsemia.com)

Edited By: Anderea Morara
Cover Concept Illustration: Robert Maina Kambo
Cover Design: Danielle Pitt
Layout Design: Kemunto Matunda

Note for Librarians:
A cataloguing record for this book is available From Library and Archives Canada.

ISBN: 978-1-926906-18-8 Paperback

Dedication

To

Eng', Risase, Huldah, Jonah, Josiah

Acknowledgements

I wish to acknowledge the efforts of the following people, who helped in the compilation of this anthology.

Charles Makari Oeri and Kennedy Ondari Ratemo who were the principal sources on the riddles.

Christopher Okemwa
December 2011

Foreword

I am delighted to write this foreward for Christopher Okemwa's ground breaking book on the Riddle as an Oral Literature genre of the Abagusii people in Western Kenya. As Okemwa ably demonstrates riddling among the Abagusii was and still is an important pedagogical tool during the formative stages of the youth. Like in many communities in Africa, Oral literature had both functional and aesthetic value for the people who consumed it. The broad genres of the oral Literature of the Abagusii include the narrative, oral poetry and the short forms of which Riddles and Proverbs are the most prominent.

Among the sub genres of the narrative forms, myth and legend served to anchor the youth to the foundational values of society. They served to link the people's social and providential needs on earth to their terrestrial and cosmic desires which in essence collapsed into the community's collective sense of being. Through myth the youth were invited to peek into the community's existential trajectory – its infinite past (*Kare na Kare*) and its infinite future – (*Kaa na Kaa*). On the other hand, the ogre and the trickster narratives, dealt with the more mundane and immediate pedagogical issues of the day such as the morality and ethics of the general populace. The production and consumption of these texts was of course nuanced with interjection (often of question nature) of discourses of the day influenced by the dominant ideology. There has been debate, for instance, on the dalliance between the ogre narrative and the society's patriarchal centredness. This does not preclude, however, the essential place these narratives held in cohering the moral and the social fabric of the community.

For the Abagusii people oral poetry was its soul. There

was poetry everywhere you listened: there was poetry at the work place, and there was poetry in ceremonies of all kinds; there was poetry in war time and there was poetry in times of peace.

Riddling which is the subject of Okemwa's book belongs to the short forms of the Gusii Oral Literature. Unlike the proverbs which were the pastime of the adults the riddles were meant to socialize children and the youth into critical thinkers by imbibing social nuances and, also, as Okemwa demonstrates, by developing a critical eye to keenly observe their physical and social environment. Children, thus, grew to understand how to encode and decode cultural codes and to (re)code these codes without undergoing through the advanced mental rigour that would be expected of them in the more intellectually challenging of the short forms: the proverbs. The witticism and diligent prodding, however, that was expected during the riddling challenges adequately prepared children for the world of proverbs and generally matriculated them to the more complex understanding of their social philosophy in adulthood. The beauty of riddling of course lies in its performance. The challenger pitches the riddle on high octane and the rest must struggle to solve it. It is not an easy ride and it never is expected. Ultimately, though, both the challenger and the respondent must be rewarded adequately. Each according to the competencies displayed.

Christopher Okemwa has again demonstrated in the publication of this book, that he has a passion for the arts and a passion for the role the arts play in chronicling appropriate technological software which make members of any society advance as civilized, creative and thinking beings.

George Obara Nyandoro
Kenyatta University, Literature Department

About the Author

Christopher Okemwa is a poet, actor, dancer, playwright, short-story and children writer. He graduated from Kamagambo Teachers' Training College and has taught for several years in Kenya. Later, joining the University of Nairobi, he obtained a Bachelor of Education degree, specializing in English and Literature; followed by Masters degree in literature from the same university. His doctoral study at Moi University in Kenya focuses on Performance Poetry in Kenya.

He has published three collections of poetry: *Toxic Love*, *The Gong* and *Purgatorius Ignis*. He has also authored three books of prose: *The Village Queen, The Visitor at the Gate, Let's Keep Tiger* and *Chubot, the Cursed One & Other Stories*.

Okemwa is recognized as an international performance poet. He attended a drama workshop in London in 1991, sponsored by NODA. He also attended a poetry workshop in Northern Ireland in 1993 sponsored by Poets' House. In 2010 he read and perfomed his poems at XX International Poetry Festival in Medellin, Colombia.

Okemwa has won several awards in poetry. In 2002 he won an Editor's Choice Award for Outstanding Achievement in Poetry, presented by the International Library of Poetry. In 2006 he won Changamoto Arts Fund Award for the performance of his poetry in Secondary Schools in Kenya. In 2010 he won Prince Claus Fund award to attend an International Poetry Festival.

By the Same Author

The Gong (poetry)

Toxic Love (poetry),
The Village Queen (short stories)
The Visitor at the Gate (short stories)
Let Us Keep Tiger (short stories)
Chubot , the Cursed One & Other Stories (short stories)

Table of Contents

Preface
3

Chapter 1
Introduction to Abagusii Riddles
5

Chapter 2
Performance of the Abagusii Riddles
7

Chapter 3
Social Functions of the Abagusii Riddles.
11

Chapter 4
A Collection of Abagusii Riddles
25

Chapter 5
Answers to Riddles
55

Preface

The aim of this book is to offer one of the most important genres of the Abagusii people—riddles. This is the first book that collects and contains riddles from all parts of the Abagusii community.

The first chapter is an introduction to riddles and riddling in the Abagusii community. It explains how the challenger sets a riddle and the response he or she gets from those attempting the riddle. The second chapter examines the performance of the riddles and forms of riddles found in the Abagusii community. Chapter three highlights the social functions of the riddles. Chapter four provides a collection of the Abagusii riddles. The chapter is divided into three sections, with section one presenting easier riddles for younger children in class one; section two a little bit harder riddles which targets children in class three; and finally section three which comprises of complicated and more involving riddles which can be answered by children from class four and above. Answers to the riddles in all the sections are provided at the end of the book.

You will realize that riddles, whose sessions take place at grandmothers' huts together with narratives, are coined from the environment, and therefore can reflect a society in which we live and also depict the historical activities and events of the community.

Chapter 1

Introduction to Abagusii Riddles

Children in the Abagusii community love to set riddles to one another. In telling a riddle, the challenger describes something, thereby giving some clue, but conceals it, leaving room for listeners to think and search for the answer. Then he or she will ask them what he or she has described. They give various answers, some very close to, and some far from, what he had described, till one of them gets the closest or the right answer.

A riddle in Ekegusii is called *embachero*; or, in plural, *chimbachero*. But when children are setting the riddles for one another the challenger starts by saying, "getandawili" (a corruption of the Kiswahili term for riddle: "kitendawili") and those listening say "tega", just as follows:

Challenge: *Getandawili*

Response: *Tega*

After they have all responded *"Tega"* the challenger goes ahead and sets his or her riddle. The one who knows the answer shouts it for all to hear and judge. If all of them give wrong answers, they ask the challenger to tell them the answer to his or her riddle. When he or she gives the answer, that answer is scrutinized by others to see how close it relates to what he or she had described in the riddle. They will eventually approve the answer. The following is an example of a challenge and a response:

Riddle: *Siomasiomi nabiroche.*(Peeps, peeps: he is spying).

Answer: *Omoibi.*(Thief.)

To get an answer to the above riddle, listeners have to think who, or which kind of person peeps and spies upon others. Some will give "God" as an answer, while others will say "The witch." They will continue making guesses, until someone will come very close, and even utter the answer: "Thief." That is the one who would have got it right.

Chapter 2

Performance of the Abagusii Riddles

In olden days riddles were performed among children in grandmother's hut. The sessions took place between supper and time for sleeping. Riddles were performed as a prelude to stories, which went on to the night, or until each child had dosed off and fallen asleep.

These days time for riddling has been taken up by school activities. Children spend more time with their teachers at school, and the role of grandmothers to lead the children in riddling has been invaded by formal schooling. Also we don't have grandmothers and their grandchildren sleeping in the same huts as before since most children, due to modern life and changing lifestyles, live with their parents, sometimes far away in urban areas. The grandmothers' role has been taken over by teachers and parents. However, riddling goes on in schools among lower primary schools and this usually offers interesting sessions.

Forms of Abagusii Riddles

Declarative Riddles: These are riddles that are descriptive in nature. The challenger describes an object, an action, or a type of person, but conceals her or his answer by avoiding coming very close to it in his or her description. For example:

Challenger: *Ande onsi ase ngochia goika gentunye/ gentunyane.* (It follows me wherever I go.)

Response: *Omorengari oo.* (One's shadow.)

The child listening to the above riddle will be made to think hard in unraveling the answer to it. He or she will ask herself the following questions: What follows someone wherever he or she goes? The possible answers can be: a dog, a friend, one's clothes, one's shoes, one's hands, one's body or one's legs. But these are obvious things which cannot be tested on. So the answer must be something else. Can the answer then be "thoughts?" "Thoughts" follow a person wherever he goes. But then "Thoughts" are an abstract thing which can not be suitable for testing. Therefore "shadow" remains a suitable and correct answer when compared to all others.

Ideophonic Riddles: These are riddles that use words that imitate the sound (of the event) they refer to; their meanings are expressed or told in the sounds made by words used in the riddle. Let us examine the following two riddles:

1. *Trrrrrr! Alo! Alo! Ng'ai ore?* (Trrrrrr! Hallo! Hallo! Where are you?)
2. *Chagara Chagara po!* (Chagara chagara po!)

What is the answer to the first riddle? Can you guess the answer going by the sound of the riddle given? The answer is: Mobile phone. The sound Trrrrr is made by a mobile phone. It is into the phone someone says the words: "hallo! hallo! Where are you?"

What is the answer to the second riddle? Do you want to guess? What makes the sound "chagara chagara" then "po!"? The answer is: A match box and a match stick. You shake the match box to first find out if it contains sticks, thereby making the sound "chagara chagara," then you open it and take out one stick and run it on the box. It explodes into a flame by making the sound "Po!" as in the riddle. Ideophonic riddles are easy to respond to since they give a sound of an object from the surrounding that one can recognize.

Interrogative Riddles: Some of the Abagusii riddles are set in the form of a question. They ask questions about an object as opposed to describing it. Let us examine the following two riddles:

3. *Kaa gento ki, gekogenda bokia na boira?* (What walks all days and all nights without stop?)
4. *Kaa nyomba ki etagoutwa?* (What house in which fire is never lit?)

The above riddles ask questions. The first one asks for something that walks day and night without stop. The answer is: The River. It is the river that goes on day and night. It never stops at nightfall or stop to rest at any time. For the second question, the answer is: The Grave. It is in the grave where fire cannot be lit, yet it houses the deceased. Riddles in form of questions provoke children into thinking, leading them to observe keenly their surroundings and arrive at an answer.

Alliterative Riddles: Some riddles are alliterative in nature. They use words whose first sounds, or letters, are the same. They also make use of assonance to give them beauty and rhythm when uttered. Let us examine the following two examples:

Riddle: *Nyaboke 'bana banchete* (Nyaboke, the one children love.)

Answer: *Egetamutamu* (Sweet.)

Riddle: *Asika esikati* (Asika, the skirt.)

Answer: *Ribururu.* (Grasshopper.)

The first riddle, *Nyaboke 'bana banchete*, has consonant <u>b</u> at the beginning of the last two words. This creates alliteration, and helps to set a chain of sounds that are sweet to the ear. This gives the listener a sense of musicality as well as making it easy to remember. Also its answer--*Egetamutamu*—creates assonance; the vowel <u>u</u> and the consonant <u>m</u> appear twice in the word and therefore creates a rhythm. The second riddle, *Asika esikati*, has sound <u>s</u> running through and connecting the two words. The vowels <u>i</u> and <u>a</u> appear in the two words, therefore creating assonance. Even the riddle's answer—Ribururu-- creates assonance. The vowel <u>u</u> and the consonant <u>r</u> in the word are repeated and are close to each other, and threfore create rhythm that echoes the riddle *Asika esikati*.

Chapter 3

Social Functions of Abagusii Riddles

Riddles serve a big purpose in the Abagusii community. The Abagusii children who use them benefit from them in many ways.

Riddles and a Child's Intellectual Ability.

Riddles make children think hard, thus enhancing their intellectual ability. In trying to find an answer to a given challenge, a child's thinking and way of reasoning is improved upon. A child develops and perfects his or her reasoning, judgement, evaluation and observation skills. The following are examples of simple riddles that don't require a lot of thinking:

Challenge: En*yomba yane tebwati gesieri.* (My house has no door.)

Response: *Rigena ri'engoko.* (An egg.)

Challenge: *Kaa gento ki, gekogenda bokia na boira?* What keeps going day and night?)

Response: *Amaache a rooche.* (River Water.)

Also we have riddles that are difficult to unravel. This category needs a lot of thinking. It requires children with sharp minds who will explore various objects, situations and descriptions and relating them to the set riddle.

The following is an example of difficult riddles meant for children from middle primary classes that need a little bit of thinking:

Challenge: *Nimbwate omosigari otari korusia gobia kagokora emeremo.* (I have a policeman who doesn't take off his cap when working.)

Response: *Omosumari.* (Nail.)

Challenge: *Nachire goaka erori yane omorero, yangire gwoka. Omonto omoao ochire koyeaka, yokire.* (I have tried to start the engine of my car, but have failed; someone else has tried and succeeded in starting the engine.)

Response: *Obotigatigi. Nabwetigatigia, togoseka.*
(Being tickled. You can't laugh if you tickle yourself, but will laugh if someone else did it to you.)

We have a category of complex riddles. This category needs sharp children in middle or upper classes of primary school to unravel. The children must be attentive and listen carefully when the challenger sets the riddle. They also must be the observant type, the quick ones in thinking. This kind of riddles require that the challenger repeats his or her riddle twice or thrice so that those listening can understand the description before they embark on finding an answer to it. He or she will repeat the riddle carefully without changing the wordings. The following two are examples of complex riddles:

Challenge: *Okondo agachia gotunya Omache, Omache agatanga goika bw'Okondo, Okondo ataraika bw'Omache.* (Okondo was following Omache, but Omache reached at Okondo's home before Okondo reached at Omache's home.)

Response: *Omonto okorina atwe ritunda. Ataraika ase ritunda, omote onyegera erinde ritunda riagwa 'nse.*
This refers to someone who is climbing up a fruit tree. Before he could reach the fruit, the tree shakes and the fruit falls down to the ground. (It touches the ground where he climbed from before he reaches the branch on which the fruit was hanging from.)

Challenge: *Minto nigo tore abamura batano babere. Babere bakanyora egechure, babere bagakeminyokia, babere bakageita, oyomo agakeria. Nintwe ng'o?*
In our family we are seven boys. Two of us found an antelope, two of us chased it, two of us killed it, and only one of us ate it. Who are we

Response: *Amaiso akarora egechure. Amagoro agakeminyokia. Amaboko akageita. Omonwa ogakeria.*
(The eyes saw the antelope. The legs chased it. The hands killed it. The mouth ate it.)

Abagusii Riddles and Development of Children's Observation Skills and Sense of Awareness.

Everyday at home children encounter objects, such as fire, soil, furniture, needle and lamp. These make up the stuff of riddles and riddling. Therefore through riddling a child gets to know his surroundings and how the objects relate to one another. The following three are examples of riddles that sharpen children's observation and sense of their surroundings:

Challenge: *Ninki kebwate amagoro ane getari kogenda?*
(What has four legs, but doesn't walk?)

Response: *Emesa.* (Table.)
Challenge: *Mama botambe nigo akoibora omwana*

obwate eriso erimo. Gagokwa, naende oibora oyonde obwate eriso erimo.
(My mother always gives birth to a child with one eye. When the child dies, she gives birth to another one with one eye.)

Response: *Esindani esire, nabo naende okogora ey'ebwate engoro eyemo buna eyio.*
(A needle has one hole; if one gets lost, you buy another one, also with one hole.)

Abagusii Riddles Enable Children to Develop a Sense of Their Body Parts and Functions

The attention of the children in the Abagusii community is drawn to parts of their bodies by riddles and riddling. They learn names of different parts of their bodies, their functions and how they relate with one another through riddles. A child will learn, for example, that even if the nape is important and holds the head in place one will never get to see it. He will also realize that no matter how much one tries he or she may not be able to count the number of hairs on his or her head. These simple facts add knowledge and stimulate curiousty in a child, thus compelling the child to observe his/her body so as to learn more. Let us take the following two riddles as examples:

Challenge: *Nintugete chiombe chinyinge, korende tinanyagoteema gochibara.*
(I have many cows, but I have never tried to count them.)

Response: Etukia. *Tinanyagotema kobara etukia yane.*
(Hair: I have never tried to count my hair).

Abagusii Riddles Promote Desirable Habits and Practices Among Children.

Certain riddles satirize and ridicule bad habits among children. Examples of the bad habits include lack of cleanliness, eating too much, having a running nose or urinating in bed. The following riddle is an example that ridicules one negative habit among children.

Challenge: *Nankio korwa Nyakongo*
(Every time coming from Nyakongo.)

Response: *Amamiria akorwa chimioro.*
(Running nose; a nose oozing mucus.)

The above riddle ridicules a child whose nose is running and does not keep him/herself tidy. Children with running noses disgust others whom they play with and hence the riddle is used to correct the habit. Riddles like this one make others sneer at them, and condem them for their untidiness.

The bahaviour of our animals is also ridiculed in riddles. When hens, goats and cows copulate publicly children shy away from them. These actions embarrass them, as much as they embarrass everyone watching the actions of these animals. Riddles are used to ridicule their actions. Let us examine the following example:

Challenge: *James gakoega, rikuba ndimoriete naende nabo akonagwasimora.*
(When James seduces a girl, he normally has a cold and sneezes.)

Response: *Egoree ekero ekobwata chimbori nigo ekobuga, "Bebebeee, tie!" buna omonto orire rikuba ogwasimora.*

(When the he-goat mates he makes the sound, "Bebebeee,tie!" sounding like someone suffering from a cold and who sneezes.)

Riddles Inform of the Socio-Economic Activities of the Abagusii Community.

The future generations of children will be informed about the social-economic activities of our community through the riddles we presently use and document. When they will study these riddles they will learn from them the things that will refer directly or indirectly to the socio economic activities that we are involved in. Let us look at the following riddle:

Challenge: *Moronge nyangoro inye.* (Moronge, the four-holed.)

Response: *Obokombe bw' chieri.* (The ox plough.)

The above riddle tells of the economic activity of the Abagusii people: farming.TheAbagusii plough their farms using *richoki* fixed and pulled along by oxen. This kind of farming currently rarely takes place because the land parcels have become too small and thus not suitable for oxen ploughing. In future, our children may learn about this activity from these written riddles.

In connection to socio-economic activities, riddles also can tell of the foods planted and eaten by our community. Abagusii plant and eat potatoes, maize and beans. They also keep cows for milk and blood. These foods are woven into riddles told by children from the Abagusii community. Examine the following two examples:

Challenge: *Kaa nyeni ki, gochire enyanyeni ime, neturekwa chitagoiteka?*
(What vegetables cannot pour out even when you overturn the pot in which they are?)

Response: *Amabere are enyari ime.* (Milk in the udder.)

Challenge: *Konagotiga aaria, ninki gwacha gokora aiga?*
(But I left you over there--what have you come to do here?)

Response: *Risosa. Kero kende nigo rikoranda gochia are; erinde riamanya kobekera amato aroro. Aye orora ng'a n'aaria rikare, ko'gochia korabia aiga, kwaributora korwa ase rimererete. Kwamanya koriboria igo.*

(The Bumpkin vines. A bumpkin vine spreads far, and can be cut accidentally because one may not know where it starts from, i.e where the roots are.)

The first riddle informs us that the Abagusii people keep cows from which they get milk. The second one indicates that bumpkin is a part of the vegetables grown by the community.

Riddles Provide an Inventory of Common Objects or Items, Dominant Activities and Popular Ideas in Specific Eras of the Abagusii Community.

In connection with socio-economic activities, riddles do tell the community's most prevalent activities, commonly-found objects and popular ideas. Objects, ideas and activities that are dominant are often referred to in riddles. An object, activity, or an idea referred to by many riddles can obviously be a common object, dominant activity, or popular idea. For instance a needle is a very common object in the Abagusii community and almost every household has one, or use one. And because children are always in contact with it, it is easy to coin various riddles about it. The following two riddles refer to a needle:

Nachire mbwatie (I am going. Follow me.)
Omosongo nyariso rimo (A one-eyed European.)

A matchbox and its sticks are also common objects found in homes. They are used by mothers regulary and children are in contact with them all the time. Familiarity with an object is what leads children to think of more and more riddles to coin from it. The following three riddles refer to the match box and sticks:

Eng'ombe yane ekero yatwereirwe teri gokamwa.
(When my cow has been rained on it cannot be milked.)

5. *Chagara Chagara pa!* (Chagara chagara pa!)
6. *Kaa mote ki ogotaroka?* (A wood that explodes.)

Children help lit fire in the evenings. They sit there helping with cooking and also get a chance of warming themselves. Fire and smoke are two objects they are most acquinted with. This is because they see it most often. Becase of this exposure to fire and its smoke children in the Abagusii community have coined numerous riddles that refer to them. The riddle below refers to fire and smoke:

7. *Kaa mogaka ki oikaransete nyomba, chimbuche chiaye chikare gotara isiko?* (Which old man, while seated in the house, has his grey beard strolling outside?)

Children, when playing at the fields, when grazing cattle,

when fetching water at the river, and when walking along the roadside coming home, love to throw sticks into the air, or at birds, or at flying aeroplanes or simply for fun. They do so to discover their effects on the object aimed at or how far the sticks will go, etc. They watch with excitement as the sticks go through the air and vanish. These sticks never return to them. Since stick-throwing is a common activity done by children, they have come to capture this activity in riddles. The riddle below refers to the activity of throwing sticks into the air by the children.

Narutire omoengwe one bwangire koirana.
(I hurled a stick away, but it has refused to return.)

Abagusii Riddles Provide Humour and Entertainment among Children

Since riddles are derived from the environment, they seem to appeal and are understood by those who live in that community. They define those people's values and norms. They express their fears, hopes and aspirations. The outsider may not catch an intended humour, a serious idea, or a cultural norm which a given riddle is trying to express or bring forth; whereas a member of that community may not miss the joke or idea being expressed, or fail to understand the sense of humour in a set riddle. What might look a plain statement, question or a mere description to someone from outside the Abagusii community, would sound amusing to the member of that community. For example there are so many riddles referring to *ugali (maize meal),*which is a staple food for the Abagusii. I think this is because the community derives its humour from eating ativities. It is not quite understood why people find food and an act of eating to be amusing. Probably it is because it is associated with the gluttons or lazy individuals. The Abagusii community values people who are not food-minded, but those who work and produce food; those who can use their time in serving others, and those who bring forth useful ideas that can help the community. The community therefore associates food, eating and drinking activities to lazy, good-for-nothing people. It is therefore during eating that humour emerges and comes out from the people. Let us examine the following riddles that are used to relate humour during community gatherings:

Riddle:	**Answer:**
Eyemo eyemo goika Bosongo (Step by step, up to Bosongo.)	*Obokima ne'ching'ende* (Ugali and beans.)
Tata emore (Father is huge.)	*Rirabwoni* (Sweet potato.)
Ting'i ting'i ombegera (Ting'i ting'i fetch it for me.)	*Obokima n'enyama* (Ugali eaten with meat.)
Twateekire omopira, suka gocha toakerane. (We have set the ball, move closer we play.)	*Endagera yabekirwe emesa, nchwo toragere.* (Food has been served, come we eat.)

The first riddle, *Eyemo eyemo goika Bosongo,* is demonstrating the eating of beans. When one chews a bean after the other, it indicates carefulness; one is careful not to eat too fast and have a false feeling that one is satisfied. Since one wants to eat a lot then one has to eat one bean after the other. A member from the Abagusii community will see ridicule in the riddle. It is intended to create humour by ridiculing the habit of some members who intend to eat a lot by carefully throwing one bean after the other into their mouths.

The second riddle, *Tata emore* (father is huge) exaggerates the bigness of a potato by referring to it as *emore* (huge) or massive or enormous. Since the potato is huge one wonders how a human being is going to eat and finish it. The person eating it then must be a monster. You can see ridicule and sarcasm in this.

The last riddle, *Twatekire omopira, suka gocha toakerane* (we have set the ball, move closer we play) satirises the eating habit. This riddle equates eating to kicking a ball. The latter involves kicking, running and shoving one another and is therefore a heavy work. Eating food is equated to that kind of heavy work. But since we know eating is not as heavy a task as football, it is a way of ridiculing those who eat with gusto.

Riddles Tell of the Technological Advancement of the Abagusii Community at Particular Periods in History.

A group of riddles studied closely can inform children of the technological level of the Abagusii community at a particular period in history. Riddles derive their material from the environment and therefore are likely to refer or contain materials that are currently available in the community at that time in history. Let us examine the following two examples:

Riddle:	*Answer*
Ndigererie ngotebie (Look at me I tell you something.)	*Riuko.* (A letter.)
Alo! alo! Ng'ayi ore? (Hallo! Hallo! Where are you?)	*Esimi ya'koboko* (Mobile phone.)

The first riddle depicts a community where Internet and mobile phones were not available; and letter writing was the form of communication by the time when the riddle was coined. The second riddle is about a mobile phone. It makes reference to how people talk on mobile phones since the gadget came into existence. Therefore we can infer that the riddle was coined more recently.

The following two riddles are set far apart in history.

Riddle: *Kaa gento ki, gekorwa nka kere nchara, gekoirana kiaigotire goika omonwa?*
(What leaves home hungry, but comes back full to the mouth?)

Answer: *Enyongo egochierwa roche. Yairwa ere enyomo, yairanigwa geichire.*
(Pot. It is taken to the river when empty, and is brought home full.)

Riddle: *Mina amato ane, inkorokere amache.*
(Twist my ears; I will vomit water for you.)

Answer: *Egetacho ki'amache.*
(Tap.)

The first riddle talks about a pot. This depicts a community set in the old times, or one found in the rural area. It is in rural areas where people fetch water from the river; thereby using pots. The second riddle is coined in the modern times where children use tapped water.

Riddles Aid in Memory

Riddles are told over and over and since their answers are more or less fixed, the children tend to cram them. Each time a riddle is set a child goes through the process of recalling the answer that was given for it in previous sessions and supplies the same. This mastery of responses to given riddles sharpens a child's skill of remembering or recalling.

Riddles Help in Socializing Children.

Riddles' sessions are a meeting point for children in the family, clan, or community. The session provides a forum on which they express themselves, display their intellectual ability, display their oratorical skills, and above all, create time for fun. Through humourous riddles children join others in laughter, amusement and enjoyment. Through riddles that ridicule they come together to sneer and jeer at negative habits and practices that prevail among them or in the community as a whole. Riddling also enables children to learn to relate to one another, respect each other, and

Brancisca Moraa of Bogiakumu Location, Kisii County, with her grandchildren—Eng', Jonah, Josiah, Hulda and Risase: Grandmothers in the Abagusii community bring their grandchildren together for riddling.

learn to be kind to others. On the whole, riddles help in the socialization process of the community.

The riddles we have collected here may not be the same in all areas of Abagusii community. Those I collected in Nyaribari, or in Bogirango maybe different from those collected in Bonchari, or in Bogetutu, or in Bobasi. I have brought all these riddles together here so that all the Abagusii children will learn and benefit from a variety of them regardless of what part of the Abagusii community they come from.

I realize that riddles are derived from the immediate environment and they keep growing every day. Children growing up in years to come will have different riddles from what we have today because theirs will be a different age and a different environment. But if we keep these ones in written form the future generation will use them to learn of the life, environment and objects used by this present generation. They will learn important facts in the history of the Abagusii people.

Chapter 4

A Collection of Abagusii Riddles

Now it is time for children, and adults alike, to test their skill in riddling by providing answers to the following riddles. The riddles are divided into three sections.

Section one is comprised of simple riddles to be responded to by children in lower primary school, standard one. The riddles use materials that class one pupils are likely to have come across. Abstract objects like wind, thoughts, feelings and others like these, are excluded.

Section two is comprised of a little bit harder and involving riddles meant to be answered by children in class three. This section uses materials that children don't have close acquaintance with. These are things found outside the homes such as the rivers, fields and markets. In this section children have to crack their brains a little and challengers should accept answers that are close to the intended meaning, since most riddles may have more than one answer.

Section three is comprised of complicated and more elaborate riddles that are long in length and whose answers require explanations. This category is meant for children in class four and above.

The riddles are meant to test a child's ability to think and provide a solution to a given complex problem. The child in this category must have experiences of crossing rivers, know types of trees in the forest, imagine the mystery of the nights, forests, dangerous animals, etc.

All the three sections have arranged their riddles in alphabetical order. The answers to all riddles are provided at the end of the book.

Section One

A

1. *Aa, to!*
Aa, to!

2. *Abagaaka nyambuche mbare minto.*
(There are old men with grey hair at our home.)

3. *Abamura abarwani bakuna ekerandi na Keminyo abugia ekerori.*
(The fighting boys touch a gourd, while Keminyo blows the pipe.)

4. *Abana bakoiborwa ne'chianga.*
(Children who are born wearing clothes.)

5. *Abana ba tata abaange, bagotara botuko rioka.*
(My father's many children walk only at night.)

6. *Abana b'Omare nigo bakoragera marara.*
(Omare's children feed while sleeping)

7. *Abang'ina barabwo n'amaroba bagosia.*
(The women are grinding soil.)

8. *Abasongo nkorwana bare ne'chimbuche.*
(White people are fighting with grey beard.)

9. *Agachia kogwa mbaro, agapiacha.*
(It landed in a place, grew big inside the place, then could not come out.)

10. *Agokwa naende oboka.*
(He dies, then comes back to life.)

11. *Aka akacha torigererie igoro.*
(Kick Akacha so that we look up to the sky.)

12. *Aka Okero, origererie igoro.*
(Kick Okero, then look up.)

13. *Alo! alo! Ng'ayi ore?*
(Hallo! Hallo! Where are you?)

14 *Amarinda taiti n'egobia nyagetaro.*
(A tight skirt and a swinging hat.)

15. *Amauga isiko, chinyama ime.*
(Bones outside; flesh inside.)

16. *Ande onsi ase ngochia goika gentunye.*
(Wherever I go it must follow me.)

17. *Ase gekoriera, nao kegosokeria.*
(It eats and excretes through the same opening.)

18. *Asika esikati.*
(Asika the skirt.)

B

1. *Baba abwate amang'ere.*
(Grandma has rough scales.)

2. *Baba mbereke.*
(Mummy, carry me on your back.)

3. *Bagaaka mbare kegoro giaito bagotenga bakoinamereria.*
(There are old men at our hill who dance and stoop.)

4. *Bakariii! Naagachire enyomba yane etari gesieri, etari tirisa.*
(*Bakariii!* I have built a house with no door, no window.)

5. *Beka ensara yao inse, torasere omonwa.*
(Put away your arrow; let us shoot using the mouth.)

C

1. *Chagara chagara po!*
(Chagara Chagara po!)

2. *Chieng'ata bw' Oroko.*
(Oroko's thin and starved one.)

3. *Chierusa mosanonoku.*
(Chierusa, the delicious one.)

4. *Ching'ondi korwa Nyakongo.*
(Sheep from Nyakongo.)

5. *Chinsoko chiaito chikare ekegoro igoro.*
(Our river sources are situated on the hillside.)

6. *Chisani ibere chireng'aine.*
(Two plates of the same size.)

7. *Chugu chugu mo!*
(Chugu chugu mo!)

E

1. *Eeri yane ekwanera egetunwa igoro k'abanto bategerera.*
(My bull bellows from the hillside attracting people's attention.)

2. *Eeri yane kemwama n'obonyoru ekare korisia ekegoro igoro.*
(My bull blackie is grazing on the hillside.)

3. *Egento nyamagoro matambe giatachire mogondo kwane.*
(An animal with long legs has stepped on my farm.)

4. *Egesagane nyamakombi omogiro.*
(A lass with rotten fermented milk.)

5. *Egetunwa nkere isikonyuma riane ntana korora; k'abande mbakerooche.*
(There is a hill behind my house. I don't see it, but others do.)

6. *Ekerandi kia baba getakwoma.*
(My mother's gourd never dries up.)

7. *Ekerandi kiane kebwate emenwa ene.*
(My milk-gourd has four mouths.)

8. *Enchera nere isikonyuma bwone, korende tinanya koyerora.*
(There is a path behind my house. I have never seen it.)

9. *Eng'ombe yane ekero yatwereirwe teri gokamwa.*
When my cow is rained on it cannot be milked.)

10. *Enyomba yane tebwati gesieri.*
(My house has no door.)

11. *Enyomba yane nigo ebwate egesigisa ekemo gioka.*
(My house is supported by one pole only.)

12. *Etaya etakorima ko maguta choi.*
(A lamp that keeps on burning, yet it has no fuel.)

13. *Etera aiga na'inche ng'etere aria toumerane bosio.*
(Go this way, I go that way; we shall meet ahead.)

14. *Etinga nyamasenyente.*
(A mill producing roughly-ground cereals.)

15. *Erongori y'omwana n'engiya.*
(A baby's porridge is good.)

16. *Esubeni nyamwamu ney'omong'ina.*
(The young black she-goat belongs to the old lady.)

17. *Eyemo eyemo goika Bosongo*
(One by one up to Bosongo.)

18. Ezeze, rikuba.
(A cough, a cold.)

G

1. *Getong'o, keriso.*
(One-eyed person.)

I

1. *Ime chinusi, isiko amanoti.*
(Coins inside, notes outside.)

2. *Inchabere inchie goteba.*
(Decorate me; I go to tell.)

3. *Inche na tata n'abamo.*
(Me and my father are one.)

K

1. *Kaa bamura ki batato oyomo ataiyo, babere tibagokora meremo?*
(Which three boys, when one is absent the other two cannot work?)

2. *Kaa gento ki, chieng'ata mok'Oroko?*
(What has a tight waistline like Oroko's wife?)

3. *Kaa gento ki, chugu chugu mo!*
(What makes the sound "chugu chugu mo!"?)

4. *Kaa gento ki, egoree nyakiagamera, esubeni nyagietina nse?*
(A he-goat that clings to; a she-goat that throws itself on the ground?)

5. *Kaa gento ki, gekogenda bokia na boira?*
(What travels day and night?)

6. *Kaa gento ki, gekoragera bokia na boira?*
(What feeds day and night?)

7. *Kaa gento ki, masiko?*
(What is always at home?)

8. *Kaa gento ki, mmmmmm?*
(What is Mmmmmm?)

9. *Kaa gento ki, nyakemini ekare ekerubo?*
(What is found in the plains and has no tail?)

10. *Kaa gento ki, sanduku pa?*
(What makes the sound "Sanduku pa!"?)

11. *Kaa gento ki, tang'ana nkorundie?*
(What is, "stay infront I drive you?")

12. *Kaa mote ki motaroka?*
(Which tree explodes?)

13. *Kaa ngori ki ntaambe, noringora etakoera?*
(Which rope is so long , that you can't finish unwinding it?)

14. *Kebusi motegereri.*
(The cat-like eavesdropper.)

15. *Keguye nganye, ng'aki ndakore nkoganye na Getembe atambea?*
(Wren, wait for me. How can I wait for you, yet Getembe is far away?)

16. *Kemite n'omosani bw'omogaka.*
(Squeeze it; it is a friend to the old man.)

17. *Kemuguri okare rogito.*
(A mound at the fence.)

18. *Kemunto ongosire.*
(Kemunto has frightened me.)

19. *Konagotiga aaria, ninki gwacha gokora aiga?*
(I left you there; what has brought you here?)

20. *Koranda koranda goika Nakuru.*
(Spreading and spreading, till you reach Nakuru.)

21. *Korigereretie Morongo, nindigereretie Sameta.*
(When you are facing Morongo, I am facing Sameta.)

22. *Korooche getogoretie nkeraire.*
(It sleeps with its eyes wide open.)

M

1. Maate ndi rogoro ndi
(Down the way it's thick, up the way it's thick.)

2. Machoronge 'mwatie
Machoronge, follow me.

4. Machoronge 'nganye
Machoronge, wait for me

4. Mankone onkoneire enyasi
(Makone has invaded the wall)

5. *Mbwate onyegerie, nong'aka ndangerie abataracha.*
(Hold me, shake me, beat me so that I call those who have not arrived.)

6. *Mobaso nondooche, botuko tondoochi. Ninche ng'o?*
(You see me during the day; at night you don't see me. Who am I?).

7. *Mokaya etera agwo, nainche ng'etere aa, tonyorane.*
(Mokaya, follow that direction; I also follow this way, and we meet.)

8. *Monda chwa!*
(Monda chwa!)

9. *Moronge nyangoro inye.*
(Moronge with four holes.)

10. *Moraa nganye.*
(Moraa, wait for me.)

11. *Mosi onyerere.*
(Mosi, the thin one.)

12. *Mosubati omwabo Chacha, nong'ainia boire nabo nkogochachania.*
(Chacha's sister, no matter how clever you are, I can still make you cry.)

13. *Moyare motengera sasati.*
(Moyare who dances in the elephant grass.)

14. *Mwa Bwana neigoire, mwa Kingi nesiekire.*
(The Boss's house is open; the King's house is locked.)

15. *Mwane nigo yasie.*
(The door to my house is open.)

16. *Mwane nyatirisa isato.*
(My house has three windows.)

N

1. *Nachire gochi maate abwo omosigari ombwatire.*
(I went down there and a policeman seized me.)

2. *Nachire maate aiga, nanyorire abang'ina bakoigusanigwa.*
(I have come down here and seen some old women shivering.)

3. *Nachiire mbwatie.*
(I have gone; follow me.)

4. *Nagesire obori botaichiri nkundi.*
(I have harvested very little finger millet; not even a handful.)

5. *Nakure korende nimbe moyo.*
(I have died, but will be alive again.)

6. *Nankio korwa Nyakongo.*
(Every day from Nyakongo.)

7. *Narutire omoengwe one bwangire koirana.*
(I have hurled a stick away, but it has refused to return.)

8. *Nche nigo nkwaa chinyeni naiyeka, nkoiyora naiyora ching'ende.*
(I cook vegetables, but what I serve is beans.)

9. *Nda! Nda! Nse bogeka. Ninki?*
(Nda! Nda! Spreading across underground. What is it?)

10. *Ndigererie ngoteebie.*
(Look at me, I tell you something.)

11. *Ng'a ngonke. Ninki?*
(Give me to suckle. What is it?)

12. *Ng'a okongo ncharokere.*
(Give me a step to help me jump over.)

13. *Ngatomera Samisoni riuko, naigure okorisoma.*
(I sent Samson a letter; I can hear him reading it.)

14. *Nigo gianchire nonde bwensi amakia aya. Ninki?*
(It is loved by everyone these days. What is it?)

15. *Nigo nkogenda tindi korigereria magega. Ninche ng'o?*
(I keep going; I never look behind. Who am I?)

16. *Nimbwate omosigari otari korusia gobia kagokora emeremo.*
(I have a policeman who doesn't take off his cap when working.)

17. *Nimbwate eredio. Ndedio ki?*
(I have a radio. What radio?)

18. *Ninde aa ninde Boraya.*
(I am here; I am in Europe.)

19. *Ninki kebwate amagoro ane getari kogenda?*
(What has four legs, but doesn't walk?)

20. *Nintugete chiombe chinyinge, korende tinanya goteema gochibara.*
(I have many cows, but I have never tried to count them.)

21. *Nkere aa nkere aaria. Ninki?*
(It is here; it is there. What is it?)

22. *Nkogena nde -- gena!*
(I wish to set a riddle? Do set!)

23. *Nkoresie emeremo.*
(Work with me.)

24. *Nokebwate korende togokerora.*
(You have it but you cannot see it.)

25. *Nokeminyokia togoikera.*
(Even if you chase it you won't catch up with it.)

26. *Nore ake onkoonie. Naye ng'o?*
(You are about to disgust me. Who are you?)

27. *Notiana boire, nabo agokobua.*
(No matter how much you defy him, he will overwhelm you.)

28. *Nsambe korwa omotwe tonsamba korwa amagoro.*
(Burn me---start with the head, not from the legs.)

29. *Ntaraigota, tingotenena.*
(If I am not full, I cannot stand up.)

30. *Ntone bwango nchie koria ebirasi.*
(Decorate me quickly. I want to go to eat left over food.)

31. *Nyabagasa egetiro.*
(Maddening speed up the hill.)

32. *Nyabagasa bwekobakobanirie gochia emete ime.*

(It has squirmed into the woods.)

33. *Nyaboke abana banchete.*
(Nyaboke, the one loved by children.)

34. *Nyakemini ekare korisia obonyoru ekegoro igoro.*
(The tail-less is grazing up on the hillside.)

35. *Nyakenywa obimbire, na bamura bamwabo nkwomana bare.*
(Nyakenywa is swollen; while his brothers are quarellling.)

36. *Nyamoncha nigo agokwa masogota.*
(Nyamoncha dies when in a supine position.)

37. *Nyantika na Mochangera omwabo.*
(Nyantika and his brother, Mochangera.)

38. *Nyansiaboka egetiro.*
(He is an up hill sprinter).

39. *Nyariansa nigo atatire. Ning'o otatete ng'o?*
(The one with a tooth missing is well-supported. Who is suppoting who?)

40. *Nyanyenya roma osimore.*
(The one with a big gap between his teeth, bite and uproot.)

41. *Nyarinda echobore togende.*
(Nyarinda take off your clothes then we go.)

echabore

O

1. *Oboremo bwaito n'omweremo omweya; totareme, totarisie.*
(Our piece of land is flat and gentle; but we can't plant on it, nor graze on it.)

2. *Obori bwane bokama bokamekia, korende ngachia kobogesa, tibwaichora nkundi.*
(My finger millet did very well on the farm, but when I harvested it, it wasn't even a handful.)

3. *Ogasusu nyagetaro nyakogoro komo.*
(The one-legged hare that is always walking.)

4. *Ogechi na Manyura bachura, chuuuuui! Chuuuui! Ndeeee! Ninki?*
(Ogechi and Manyura scream: "Chuuuuui! Chuuuui! Ndeee!" What is it?)

5. *Ogoto kama ndugu.*
(The frog like a brother.)

6. *Okanda nyamboyu omogonga obota*
(Small-stomached, well-clad, with a bowed back.)

7. *Okondo agachia gotunya Omache, Omache agatanga goika bw'Okondo, Okondo ataraika bw'Omache.*
(Okondo was following Omache, Omache reached the home of Okondo before Okondo reached Omache's home.)

8. *Omogaka nyaisio nomong'ina nyabong'ere.*
(An old man with a baldhead and an old woman with scaly feet.)

9. *Omoiseke nare minto okweyaka amaguta boira.*
(There is a girl in our home who applies oil on her skin every day.)

10. *Omoiseke nyaikobu iseera.*
(A girl with a beautiful navel.)

11. *Omoiseke okorabia okona gotera.*
(A girl who sings while slashing.)

12. Omorendi otari gokwana.
(A watchman who doesn't talk.)

13. Omomura otakorusia tai igoti.
(A youngman who never removes his neck-tie.)

14. *Omong'ina enkara.*
(A shrivelled old woman.)

15. Omong'ina nyamachanchabe akoroma.
(An old woman whose tattered clothes bite.)

16. Omong'ina nyanyenche okare gotuma ribina ekerubo.
(A decorated old woman dancing in the plains.)

17. Omong'ina okorera rikori gotira.
(An old woman crying as she walks up the pathway.)

18. Omororia o'Nyamwaka.
(Nyamwaka's whistling).

19. *Nyabagasa emete ime.*
(A wonderer in the woods.)

20. *Omosongo obwatire enyigo.*
(A whiteman stands akimbo.)

21. Omwana bw'Omosongo ore ekerasi ime.
(A whiteman's child in a pod.)

22. Ondari osibire etai.
(Ondari has tied his neck-tie.)

23. *Onduso nyamotwe.*
(Big-headed Onduso)
24. *Ongori nyariansa.*
(Ongori, with a tooth missing.)

25. *Onkombi orogunchara.*
(Thick milk in a horn.)

26. *Onsase nyariso riomo.*
(The tough-eyed Onsase.)

27. *Onsinini Onsinini kononchanda.*
(Tiny tiny yet it is a nuisance.)

28. *Ontong'ino onsinini, nabo agokoreria.*
(Ontong'ino is tiny but will make you cry.)

29. *Ontune ontune.*
(A delicate, delicacy.)

30. *Opopo kenyansa siruari bikwendo.*
(Huge, clad in a pair of burly shorts.)

P

1. *Peni nyakoboko komo.*
(One-handed Peni.)

R

1. *Randa, randa, siomeria gocha isiko.*
(Spread, spread, then peep out.)

S

1. *Sabina otererire.*
(Sabina is slippery.)

2. *Sabina rikondo.*
(Sabina the loud speaker (That part of public address system that the sound comes out of).)

3. *Saga saga mokera, wa wa.*
(Saga saga mokera, wa wa.)

4. *Sani karanda karanda chireng'aine.*
(Sprawling like two same-size huge plates.)

5. *Seremani ogundirie emete.*
(The carpenter who has made trees to rot.)

6. *Simeka, simora, simeka, simora.*
(Plant, uproot, plant, uproot.)

7. *Sindake moyio.*
(A needle, like a knife.)

8. *Sindake omonwa.*
(With a needle-size mouth.)

9. *Sinsi ndwanie.*
(The tiny one, fight me.)

10. *Siomasiomia nabirooche.*
(Peeping, peeping; he is spying on them.)

11. *Sista okare o Martini.*
(Sister at Martin's.)

12. *Sukuru komiti.*
(School committee.)

13. *Susana morema motegereri.*
(Susana, the digger, the eavesdropper.)

T

1. *Tangatanga Bonchari, Kamagambo, Nairobi mboeto.*
(Wander through Bonchari, Kamagambo, Nairobi---everywhere.)

2. *Tata egetankumba, baba ogoaka amaguta.*
(My father is bent at work, my mother is applying oil.)

3. *Tata emore.*
(My father is a big mound!)

4. *Tata nabwate ebirogo bibere, ekemo gechabeire amandere, n'ekende getachabeiri.*
(My father has two chairs; one is decorated, the other is not.)

5. *Tata nyagutwa mbariri ekoengecha motwe.*
(My father has a dancing crown on his head.)

6. *Tata obwatire epigipigi gochia Getembe.*
(My father is on his motorbike to Getembe.)

7. *Tata ogure n'egoti yaye.*
(My father has fallen down with his coat.)

8. *Tata osibire etai gochia Kemera.*
My father has tied his neck-tie and gone to Kemera.

9. *Tonachera etigiti ekerogo igoro, yaa.*
(Don't leave a ticket on the chair, youngman.)

10. *Twatekire omopira, suka gocha toakerane.*
(We have set the ball; come we play.)

Section Two

A

1. *Abagaka baikaransete n'abang'ina bakorwana.*
(Old men are seated while old women are fighting.)

2. *Abaiseke mbare minto batato oyomo ataiyo ntokoragera.*
(There are three sisters in our house. When one of them is absent we can't have something to eat.)

3. *Abana bane babere bagokora egasi batari goikana ang'e.*
(My two children work together, but never come to close contact.)

4. *Amina mina mina, achwata chwata chwata.*
(He weaves, weaves, weaves; then stretches, stretches, stretches.)

5. *Ara egesero toriere chinsobosobo.*
(Spread the hide we eat gooseberries on it.)

C

1. *Chichabi chi'Omonso chigerekaine.*
(Omosa's latches are intertwined.)

E

1. *Ebundi karakara.*
(A quick artisan).

2. *Engori otaringe.*
(A rope you can't fold.)

3. *Ekegogwa chamabunduki n'esurwari bikwendo.*
(A comb on the head, a pair of shorts below.)

4. *Ekemoni nyamokombotoria.*
(A cat with claws.)

5. *Enchera ya Nyamoniambo onde tana koyeeta, n'ere bweka.*
(No one has ever trod on Nyamoniambo's path; except him alone)

6. *Enchera yane ntori gosanga nonde.*
(I don't share my path with anybody.)

7. *Engoko yane nerarerete amagwa ime.*
(My hen is incubating eggs in the thorny bush.)

8. *Engoko yane yabiareire amagwa ime.*
(My hen has laid eggs in the thorny bush.)

9. *Enyomba yaito machani omorobini, nyakona inye, eichire amabere.*
(Our house is green, has four corners and full of milk.)

J

1. *James gakoega, rikuba ndimoriete.*
(When James is seducing a girl; he usually has a cold.)

K

1. *Kaa gento ki, gekoriera omonwa giasookeria rikere?*
(It feeds through the mouth, excretes through its sides.)

2. *Kaa gento ki, gekorwa nka kere nchara, gekoirana kiaigotire goika omonwa?*
(It leaves home hungry; it comes back fully fed. What is it?)

3. *Kaa gento ki, getagosika para ya Mosongo?*
(It has no respect for a whiteman's path. What is it?)

4. *Kaa mogaka ki, ogoteera omanya gosaa mwaye?*
(Which old man sings, then diarrhoeas in his house?)

5. *Kaa momura ki otari na'nengo*
(A boy with no joints.)

6. *Kaa nyeni ki, gochire enyanyeni ime, neturekwa chitagoiteka?*
(Which vegetable cannot drop out even when you oveturn the cooking pot.)

7. *Kaa nyomba ki, etagoutwa?*
(A house in which no fire is lit.)

8. *Kabakaba ebituma biombera.*
(It makes the sound "*kabakaba*" in the maize plantation.)

M

1. *Mama, botambe nigo akoibora omwana obwate eriso erimo. Gakure, naende oibora oyonde obwate eriso erimo.*
(My mother gives birth to children who have one eye. When a child dies, she again gives birth to another one with one eye.)

2. *Mbo! Mbo! Ngokwa nde!*
(*Mbo! Mbo!* I am dying!)

3. *Mbwatesie Moraa tokore egasi buya.*
(Assist me, Moraa, so we can effectively work together.)

4. *Minto tindi koria bokima n'erongori nkonywa. Ninche ng'o?*
(At my home I don't eat ugali; I drink porridge only. Who am I?)

5. *Mokogoti ntweke nainche ngotweke.*
(Help me put it on my head; I will also help you put it on your head.)

6. *Mokoko kwang'ita!*
(*Mokoko*, you are killing me.)

N

1. *Naigure Kwamboka okwanora amao.*
(I can hear Kwamboka gathering hides together.)

2. *Nachire gokuna omwana obande okure.*
(I have touched someone's child and he has died.)

3. *Nachire gosooka isiko, nanyorire nyang'era.*
(I bumped into a buffalo as I was going out of my house).

4. *Nanyorire omong'ina ogoita mayenga maate aiga.*
   (I have found an old woman dancing down there.)

5. *Nanyorire omwana obande okorera maate aiga.*
   (I have come across somebody's child crying down there.)

6. *Nanyorire Nyamisa ogotenya maate aiga.* (I have found Nyamisa collecting firewood down there.)

7. *Nanyorire omonto maate aiga, nachire komokwania, bwebundire.* (I came across someone down here; but when I greeted him he coiled.)

8. *Narorire Nyabengo okwegega.*
   (I have seen Nyambengo trudging along.)

9. *Ngatoma abana babere, bangire koirana.*
   (I sent two children out on an errand; but they have failed to return.)

10. *Ngende orogongo oroao, goika ndware nkwe. Korende kinde seito mbuya nde.*
    (If I go to a different place I'll get sick and die; but I am alright when I am at home.)

11. *Ng'ina n'omwororo, korende abana baye n'abatindi.*
    (The mother is tolerant; however, the children are fierce.)

12. *Ng'o okogosa otamanyeti.*
    (It frightens the one who does not know it)

O

1. *Oiboire omwana otari maboko, otari magoro, otari maiso, otari mato, otari... Mwana ki?*

(She has given birth to a child who has no hands, no legs, no eyes, no ears, and no... What child is it?)

2. *Omokungu nyabisero binge, k' abana nse akwareria.*
(She has many rugs, yet her children sleep on the bare floor.)

3. *Omokungu nyamaboko atato. Ninki?*
   (A woman with three hands. What is it?)

4. *Oyokorosia tagetageti; oyogokeira tagetageti.*
   (It is disliked by the one who makes it; and hated by the one who takes it.)

R

1. *Randa randa Simioni.*
(Spread, spread, Simion.)

T

1. *Tegerera ngoteebie.*
(Listen, I tell you.)

2. *Ting'i ting'i ombogeria.*
(*Ting'i ting'i* give way.)

3. *Tokagenda obogeni n'omosani one, agatiga egetambaa ekerabu ekerogo igoro.*
(My friend and I were visitors at a home; when we went away he left a white handkerchief on the chair.)

Section Three

A

1. *Abamura mbare mwabo batato. Oyomo obwate chitorobini. N'oyonde obwate endege. N'oyonde obwate amariogo. Nyatorobini agapima akarora ase omoiseke akarwarete anyaregete. Nyandege akababogoria gochi-oo. Nyamariogo akaa omoiseke eriogo akagwena. Bono ning'o oraire omoiseke oyio?*
(There are three boys in a family. One with a telescope, another with an aeroplane, while the third had medicine. The one with the telescope saw a sick, dying girl at her home. The one with an aeroplane flew them to the home. While the one with the medicine cured the girl. Who should marry her?)

2. *Abanto batato ngotamboka bare roche amache; oyomo oyarigereirie nakoyatacha; oyonde tayatacheti korende oyarigereirie; oyonde tayarochi naende tayatacheti. Bonsi bambokire. Batato abwo mbarabi?*
(Three people are crossing the river; one sees the water and is walking in it; the second one is seeing the water but is not walking in it; the third one is neither seeing nor walking in the water. Who are the three?)

3. *Amatunda namete rooche gati na bwato tiboiyo. Ng'aki togokora toikere amatunda ayio?*
(A fruit-tree grows in the middle of the river. We have no boat to use to reach it. What can we do to reach the fruits?)

4. *Amanyanyimbo agokorera oboraro n'endagera ko mosara choi.*
(Policemen working for only accommodation and food; no salary paid to them.)

B

1. *Baba otindekire omena nse.*
(Grandma has buried "fish" in the ground.)

E

1. *Ekenyamagoro ane, kiarinire ekenyamagoro ane, kiaganyire ekenyamagoro ane.*
(A four-legged climbs on a four-legged, and waits for a four-legged.)

K

1. *Kaa gento ki, eng'ombe na ng'ina mori?*
(What is like the cow and its calf?)

2. *Kaa gento ki, kegosoka kiagendera amagoro ane, kegokina kiagendera abere, omoerio oye kiagendera atato?*
(It comes out walking on four legs; when it grows up it walks on two; finally it walks on three.)

3. *Kaa gento ki, getagotamboka nchera?*
(What never never goes across the road?)

4. *Kaa gento ki, kegotwata rimo rioka, erinde giakwa?*
(What gives birth only once and dies?)

5. *Kaa mogaka ki, ogotengera mwaye oka, osiomeria gesieri k'oirana?*
(Which old man only dances in his house; peeping out once in a while, but never gets out?)

6. *Kaa mogaka ki, oikaransete nyomba, chinderu chiaye chimbuche chikare gotara isiko?*
(Which old man sits in his house while his grey beard goes out for a walk?).

7. *Kaa momura ki, okogenda emeremo getirianda, okoirana ocha ne chianga?*
(Which youngman goes to work naked; but comes back dressed?)

8. *Kaa mote ki, ogosiicha mambia, magoroba ebisicha biaroroka?*
(Which tree blooms in the morning and sheds its leaves in the evening?)

9. *Kaigotete nario akorera, kare nchara nario akirete.*
(When satisfied and full he complains and cries; when hungry he calms down and doesn't complain.)

10. *Kang'ina bweakire etago.*
(The old woman has painted herself with red ochre)

11. *Kanikaka kaboora, "ntweke egetonga mayae"*
(Put a yellow basket on my head.)

12. *Ke'bikwendo ke' bitore.*
(Like a calf's swollen stomach when it has drunk water.)

13. *Kinde aa ninde Getembe.*
(I am here at the same time I am at Getembe.)

14. *Kinde ng'umbu aa, ere oikire ng'umbu eria.*
(When I am still here, he has already reached on the other side of the river.)

15. *Kinde ng'umbu eria, mwane yasie.*
(When I am far away my house is normally open.)

16. *Kinde ng'umbu eria, nindooche enchoke egochingirira mwane.*
(While on the other side of the river I can see a bee flitting around my house.)

17. *Konachire obogeni nakio kegotanga gonkwania.*
(It is the first one to greet me when I go to visit my friends.)

18. *Kwaeirwe ebara, embori n'enyang'au obiambokie gochia nyancha ng'umbu. Obwato n'obomo bwoka oire; naende goika bobogorie egento ekemo gioka amo n'aye gochia ng'umbu. Orore embori teria ebara n'enyang'au teria embori. Teeba buna orabiambokie.*
(You have been given limesalt, a goat and a hyena to carry them across the river using one boat. The boat has to carry one item with you at a time. Explain how you will carry the three items across, making sure the goat does not eat limesalt and the hyena does not eat the goat.)

M

1. *Minto nigo tore abamura batano na babere. Babere bakanyora egechure, babere bagakeminyokia, babere bakageita, oyomo agakeria. Nintwe ng'o?*
(We are seven boys in the family. Two of us came across an antelope. Two of us chased it. Two of us killed it. One ate it. Who are we?)

N

1. *Nabooria ekierigori rikong'u goika aegwe. Ning'o?*
(Even if she requests for an expensive item, she will be given. Who is she?)

2. *Nachia kogenda etuka Getembe, nanyora abasigari bagwekaine. Naende nachia kogenda etuka Nairobi, nanyora abasigari bagwekaine. Mbarabi?*
(I went to a shop at Getembe and the policemen there look alike; I went to a shop in Nairobi and the policemen there also look alike. Who are they?)

3. *Nachire goaka erori yane omorero, yangire gwoka. Omonto omoao ochire koyeaka, yokire.*
(I have tried to start the engine of my vehicle but I have failed; someone else has succeeded.)

4. *Nachire gochia maate agwo, nanyorire omosigari obegete egobia embariri burure.*
(When I went down there I saw a policeman in a very red cap.)

5. *Nyasae bwanchire gokoa eriso rikorora ande onsi; ng'ai oranche ribere?*
(God is willing to give you an eye that can see everywhere; where would you prefer it to be placed?)

O

1. *Onye nantongetwe indigereretie igoro, anga naitete abanto n'embura.*
(If I was created facing up, I could kill people with my rain.)

2. *Omwana one okure, korende ebirero n'Chache bikare.*
(My child has died; but the funeral is being held far away)

Chapter 5

ANSWERS TO RIDDLES

Section One

A

*1. Oboterere (*Sliding and falling on a slippery ground.)

2. Ememera (Yeast.)

3. Abaaki enkoyo nabwo abarwani. Enkoyo n'ero ekerandi
(Football players are the fighting boys. The gourd refers to the ball.)

*4. Chibando nyabiemba (*Maize cobs.)

5. Ching'enang'eni chia igoro chikomesa botuko rioka.
(The stars in the sky that shine only at night.)

6. Amage y'enyoni akorageriguja.
(Nestlings.)

7. Chimonyo chikorosia riumbagero.
(Ants making an anthill.)

8. Chibando chinyomo chigotoreka ekero chigokarangwa.
(Dry maize seeds spattering when they are being roasted. Cf pop corn)

9. Enda y'okogoro ekero yarenge ensona, egasineneka

omonto. Ekamonyunyunta amanyinga etachete bombaro. Omoerio oye ekaba enene, ekaresanera okogoro ime; egasinywa gosooka.
(A flea before it sucks blood and finally turns into a big round jigger on someone's foot.)

10. *Omotienyi.*
(Moon.)

11. *Aka omopira esuti toyororere igoro.*
(Kick the ball up; we see it in the sky.)

12. *Omopira.*
(Ball.)

13. *Esimi ya' koboko*
(Mobile phone.)

14. *Ekong'a enyerereete gochia nse, korende egatwara egesure.*
(A crested crane with a comb on his head.)

15. *Ebisanda bie rigena ri' engoko nabio amauga. Omochununu oye noro chinyama.*
(An egg: Its shell is the bones; the yoke is the flesh.)

16. *Omorengari .*
(Shadow.)

17. *Ekerandi ki'amabere.*
(Milk gourd.)

18. *Ribururu.*
(Grasshopper.)

B

1. *Rigena riokoora.*
(Grinding stone.)

2. *Egetanda.*
(Bed.)

3. *Obonyoru bokwongoyana ekero embeo ekogusa.*
(Long grass/thatch-grass that shakes and lies in the wind.)

4. *Engoko ko yabiarire rigena, nabo ekobuga igo.*
(When a hen lays an egg it makes the sound Bakiriii! The egg is the house with no door, no window.)

5. *Ritusia rigoteebia amagecha arome eng'ombe na konyunyunta amanyinga.*
(The big tick telling the small tick to bite a cow and suck blood.)

C

1. *Ekebiriti ogosungusia oigwe gose ebite mbireo; kwamanya korusia egete ekemo, gwaaka erinde omorero omoka ng'a po!*
(You make the sound of "chagara chagara" when shaking the match box to ensure that there are sticks. You then strike one making the sound, "Po!")

2. *Ekiaramba.*
(Wasp.)

3. *Enchugu egwansa monwa.*
(Groundnut tasting in the mouth as it is being chewed.)

4. *Amamira naro ching'ondi. Chimioro nachio Nyakongo.*
(Sheep refers to mucus. Nyakongo refers to nostrils.)

5. *Chimioro nachio chinsoko. Omotwe noro ekegoro.*
(Nostrils(river sources) are situated on the head (hillside).)

6. *Ense na igoro.*
(The earth and the sky.)

7. *Omonengwe.*
(A piece of wood/stick when flung.)

E

1. *Embura ekogukura korwa igoro.*
(Thunderstorms before the rain falls.)

2. *Chinda ch'omotwe chire ime yetukia.*
(Lice inside the hair.)

3. *Embura egotwa korwa igoro buna egento kebwate amagoro amataambe.*
(Rain. When it falls it looks like an animal with long legs.)

4. *Eriso nyabitotia.*
(An eye with white discharge at the corners.)

5. *Ekiongotiro.*
(Nape.)

6. *Enyari ye ng'ombe.*
(A cow's udder.)

7. *Enyari ye'ng'ombe*
(A cow's udder.)

8. *Ekiongotiro.*
(Nape.)

9. *Ekebiriti.*
(Match box.)

10. *Rigena ri'engoko.*
(An egg.)

11. *Oboba.*
(Mushroom.)

12. *Risase/ Erioba)*
(Sun.)

13. *Orokini gose omochibi ekero okweboyia.*
(Belt.)

14. *Ekeumbu ki' amandegere amete.*
(A clump of of small type of mushrooms.)

15. *Chitoro.*
(Sleep.)

16. *Enyanyeni omong'ina akoiyekera chinyeni.*
(The pot used by an old woman for cooking vegetables.)

17. *Obokima ne' ching'ende.*
(Ugali and beans.)

18. Enyamoreo.
(AIDS.)

G

1. Entururu ebochoire.
A coin with a hole in the middle.

I

1. Egetuma kere n'amasakara.
(A maize cob with sheathing. The seeds are the shillings while the sheathing represents notes).

2. Rirube.
(A letter.)

3. Amache n'ekerasi.
(Water and a glass.)

K

1. Amaiga ariko.
(Cooking Stones – usually three.)

2. Emonyo: ase enda yaye ebwatanerete n'egekuba nigo are anyerere buna omonto bwetingete n'orokini.
(An ant: Its narrow waistline depicts a person who has tightly tied the abdomen with a belt.)

3. Omoengwe k'orutirwe nabo okobuga igo.
(A piece of wood/stick makes this sound when thrown/hurled.)

4. Omosacha okorabia nere egoree nyakiagamera; omokungu okorema n'ere esubeni nyagietina nse.
(A man slashing and a wife digging.)

5. Amache arooche.
(A river.)

6. Enyancha ase chindooche chigosoa bokia na boira.
(The Ocean/ Lake into which rivers empty themselves day and night.)

7. Engoko emenyete nka.
(A domestic fowl/hen.)

8. Omosunte obetete igoro na nse.
(A very dark night.)

9. Egioto kemenyete ang'e na rooche. Tikebwati kemincha.
(A tail-less frog near the river.)

10. Egesanda gi'ekenagwa kegwateka boigo.
The pod containing Mauritius thorn seeds; it makes the sound "pa!" when it explodes.

11. Amabere agoteebia obokima ekero okoragera.
(This refers to what milk tells ugali when in the mouth while being eaten by someone.)

12. Ekebiriti.
(Match stick.)

13. Enchera.
(The road.)

14. Embeba egokiria yategerera koyaigure omonto.
(A rat. It keeps still when it senses danger.)

15. *Enyama ogoetaneria, egoteebia obokima boyeganye.*
(This is a reference to meat when eating it with ugali. Ugali often goes down the throat, leaving the meat behind.)

16. *Ekerangesa.*
(This is a fermented tobacco inhaled from a horn.)

17. *Omuongo.*
(Pumbkin.)

18. *Amarwa.*
(Traditional beer.)

19. *Risosa. (Kero kende nigo rikoranda gochia egeka, erinde riamanya kobeka amato aroro. Aye orora ng'a n'aaria rikare, kogochia korabia aiga, kwaributora korwa ase rimerete. Kwamanya koriomania igo)*
(Pumbkin stem and leaves.)

20. *Amarabwoni gose risosa rikoranda.*
(Sweet potato or pumbkin vines.)

21. *Amaiso arigereretie Marongo n'ekiongotira kerigereretie Sameta.*
(The eyes and the nape (back of head).)

22. *Egechure ekero keraire chitoro, amaiso aye nigo aramogetie rioka.*
(Antelope. Its eyes remain open even when it is asleep)

M

1. *Egesunte.*
(Pitch dark.)

2. Esindani egotebia eusi.
(A needle telling a thread.)

3. Amabere agoteebia obokima.
(Milk telling pieces of ugali when someone is eating.)

4. Egetangora ki' emete eminire.
(A cupboard made from twisted tree wood.)

5. Ekengere okobwata kwabugia.
(A bell that someone is ringing.)

6. Erioba rikororekana mobaso rioka.
(The sun, which is seen only during daytime.)

7. Orokini.
(A belt.)

8. Ritimo rikorutwa igo.
(A spear. It makes that sound when thrown.)

9. Richoki rigosiberwa chieri.
(The oxen yoke.)

10. Okoragera namabere.
(Eating ugali with milk.)

11. Esigara enyerereete ekonyugwa ng'oora.
(A cigarette. It is thin and usually smoked slowly)

12. Enchara egoteebia omonto ekoria.
(Hunger telling someone feeling it.)

13. Ekong'a egotengera sasati.
(A crested crane, wading through elephant grass.)

14. Etongoro ebochoire, nero mwa Bwana.Esiringi etabochoiri, nero mwa Kingi.
(A ten-cent coin with a hole and a shilling coin with no hole.)
(This arose from the fact that during colonial times the ten cent coin had a hole in the centre while the shilling coin did not have a hole, but had the king's crown.)

15. Engoro yeguto.
(An ant-bear's hole/liar.)

16. Orwembe.
(Razor blade.)

N

1. Ekenagwa.
(Mauritius thorn.)

2. Ekebabe gekwongoyana ekero embeo ekogusa.
(Napier grass shaking in the wind.)

3. Esindani egoteebia eusi.
(A needle telling a thread.)

4. Etukia.
(Hair.)

5. Nararire chitoro, korende ninche mboke.
(I have slept, but will wake up again.)

6. Amamira akorwa chimioro
(Mucus flowing from the nostrils.)

7. *Erioki ritakoirana ase omorero.*
(Smoke that billows away but does not return to the fire.)

8. *Embori ekorisia amato, yania chimbiribiri.*
(A goat that eats leaves, but excretes pellets.)

9. *Ekenyambi gekoranda amaroba ime.*
(Couch grass spreading beneath the top soil.)

10. *Egetabu okorigereria gwachaka gosoma amang'ana.*
(A book you are reading.)

11. *Orokore okobwata kwanywera amarwa.*
(A long traditional beer drinking straw.)

12. *Ng'a amabere ntirimbokerie amarabwoni.*
(Give me milk to help swallow sweet potatoes).

13. *Enswe ekoromera.*
(Fish in water eating a bait.)

14. *Chibesa.*
(Money.)

15. *Amache.*
(Water flowing in the river.)

16. *Omosumari.*
(Nail.)

17. *Obotigatigi: Abana nigo banchete gotigatigania.*
(Tickling. Kids like tickling each other.)

18. *Eredio.*
(Radio.)

19. Emesa.
(Table.)

20. Tinanya goteema kobara etukia yane.
(Hair. No one has ever attempted to count their hair)

21. Amaiso.
(Eyes.)

22. Rimama.
(Dumb person.)

23. Omorengari.
(Shadow.)

24. Ekiongotiro.
(Nape (Back of the head).)

25. Omorengari.
(Shadow.)

26. Omobaso ogwoterera korende ocha ogokoonia.
(The sun's warmth, when you have basked long enough.)

27. Enchara.
(Hunger.)

28. Egetambe gi'etaya.
(A wick.)

29. Egunia: etarabekwa ebinto teri gotenena.
(A sack. If not filled, it will not stand up.)

30. Masamu yaboorete bo.
(The hyena, out of greediness, is said to have requested so.)

31. *Embeba egotira gochia gesara.*
(A rat running up a thatched roof.)

32. *Ekegwankwa gianchete goeta emete ime ase ebisicha bire.*
(A butterfly; it loves passing through trees, especially where there are flowers.)

33. *Egetamutamu.*
(A sweet.)

34. *Enda y'omotwe.*
(A head louse, in the hair.)

35. *Embura yaingire, nero Nyakenywa obimbete. Enkoba egoaka na kogukura, nero bamura bamwabo bakwomana.*
(The rain clouds ready to burst into rain, while thunder roars.)

36. *Esobono.*
(Cockroach.)

37. *Amaruma abere akoiruruka.*
(Two doves flying.)

38. *Embeba.*
(A rat.)

39. *Ekiage kie rinyoro gesirire n'amatiro.*
(A granary supported with poles.)

40. *Enyundo egosimora emesumari.*
(A hammer, when uprooting nails.)

41. Ebando ogotwa kwayerusia amasabo onsi.
(A maize cob. You remove all its cover sheath before eating it.)

O

1. Enyancha.
(Lake/ocean.)

2. Etukia ko yagingeirwe, teri goichora koboko.
(Hair; when shaved is hardly a handful.)

3. Oboba.
(Mushroom.)

4. Ritimbo rikonywera ebisicha.
(Beetle sucking juice from the flowers.)

5. Engoko n'etwoni.
(Hen and cock.)

6, *Ekiarambe*
(Wasp)

7. Omonto okorina atwe riko. Ataraika ase riko, omoko onyegera, erinde riko riagwa nse.
(Someone who is climbing up a fruit tree, shakes the tree and the fruit falls to the ground. So the fruit reaches the ground before the climber reaches for the twig on which the fruit was hanging from.)

8. Ritierio, nario omogaka nyaisio. Ribiria, nario omong'ina nyabong'ere.
(A smooth sharpening stone is the old man, while a grindingstone is the old woman with scaly feet.)

9. *Enyongo ere amache botambe.*
(A pot that always has water.)

10. *Omotienyi.*
(Moon.)

11. *Amagasi.*
(A pair of scissors.)

12. *Ekeburi.*
(Padlock.)

13. *Ribururu.*
(Grasshopper.)

14. *Ekegwesi*
(Smoking pipe.)

15. *Risami.*
(Hairy caterpillar).

16. *Ekong'a.*
(Crested crane.)

17. *Ritimbo.*
(Beetle.)

18. *Embeo ekogusa.*
(A wind blowing.)

19. *Ekegwankwa.*
(Butterfly.)

20. *Egekombe.*
(Cup.)

21. *Ensobosobo entobu.*
(A ripe gooseberry.)

22. *Ekegonkoru.*
(Crow.)

23. *Enungu.*
(Club—a short stick with one thicker and roundish side.)

24. *Ekiage g' ekenyoro.*
(A community granary.)

25. *Amamiria are chimioro.*
(Mucus in the nostrils.)

27. *Risase (Erioba).*
(Sun's rays.)

28. *Ensona. Koyakoromire nigo okoyerigia igo kwayenyora, erinde kwayerusia. Kogochia koyerigereria orora n'ensinini mono etagwenereti gokoroma bororo igo.*
(A flee. It is small but its bite is very painful, and finding it is difficult.)

29. *Egechuni kegosoa eriso.*
(A tiny insect that sometimes goes into one's eye.)

30. *Enyama.*
(Meat.)

31. *Etwoni.*
(Cock)

P

1. *Egekombe.*
(Cup.)

R

1. Amarabwoni akoranda.
(Sweet potatoes vines creeping.)

S

1. Enswe botambe kere rooche nigo ere enterere.
(Fish in the water is always slippery.)

2. Etaya y'esitima.
(Light bulb.)

3. Ekegwankwa.
(Butterfly. The sound it makes.)

4. Igoro na nse.
(Sky and earth.)

5. Ritimbo rigosegesa emete.
(Beetle gnawing at trees.)

6. Okogenda n'amagoro.
(Walking on foot.)

7. Ensagara.
(Lizard.)

8. Ekiage gekobekwa endagera.
(The granary that stores farm produce. It has a small window.)

9. Ensona.
(Flee.)

10. *Omoibi.*
(Thief.)

11. *Emonyo yetingete buna abasista baria banyagitari.*
(An ant dressed to resemble hospital nurses.)

12. *Abarogi bare omosangererekano.*
(An assembly of witches at night.)

13. *Eng'uko gekorema nigo ekoigwa egento erinde yakiria, yategerera.*
(A mole. When it senses danger while burrowing, it stays still, listening.)

T

1. *Omokungu omotaari. Riraya. Rirogo.*
(Prostitute.)

2. *Tata ogosereta. Baba okooma.*
(My father is thatching a hut, while my mother is smearing the walls.)

3. *Rirabwoni rineene.*
(A huge sweet potato.)

4. *Igoro na nse.*
(The sky and the earth.)

5. *Etwoni nyarogoncho.*
(A cock with a comb on his head.)

6. *Enyasore ekonyugwa.*
(Opium when being smoked.)

7. Ritoke riagechirwe.
(Banana plank that has been cut and felled.)

8. Ribururu.
(Grasshopper.)

9. Enkene.
(Tape worm.)

10. Endagera yabekirwe emesa, nchwo toragere.
(Food has been placed on the table; come we eat.)

Section Two

A

1. Amagena a rooche naro abagaka. Amache agoeta naro abang'ina bakorwana.
(The old men imply stones in the river, while old women refer to the passing water of the river.)

2. Amaiiga.
(Hearthstones.)

3. Amaiso.
(Eyes.)

4. Oronyambobe rokoagacha ne chiusi chiaye rogochimina na goching'usa.
(A spider making a web. He weaves the threads and then stretches them.)

5. Erioba nario egesero. Ching'enang'eni nachio chinsobosobo.
(The hide refers to the sky; the gooseberries refer to the stars.)

C

1. Richambe ribwate amauncho asoneranirie amo amo.
(A mat made from intertwined strands.)

E

1. Oronyambobe.
(Spider.)

2. Enchera.
(Road, path.)

3. Ekenagwa kegokombotoria omonto gose eyanga.
(A Mauritius thorn, holding onto someone's body or clothing.)

4. Eusi y'oronyambobe nero enchera. Oronyambobe narwo Nyamonimbo.
(The spider and its web.)

5. Eng'uko.
(Mole.)

9. Engoto.
A jojoba type of plant.

J

1. Egoree ekero ekobwata chimbori nigo ekobuga, "Bebebeee, tie!" buna omonto orire rikuba ogwasimora.
This refers to a he-goat. When it wants to mate with female goats, it makes the sound "*bebebeee, tie!*" like someone sneezing because of a cold.

K

1. Etinga y'amache.
(A water mill.)

2. Enyongo egochierwa rooche. Yairwa ere enyomo;yairanigwa eichire.
(A pot. It is taken to the river when it is empty and returned when it is full of water.)

3. Eguto ekorema ande onsi, nonya n'epara igoro.
(An Ant bear. It digs anywhere, even on the road.)

4. Ritimbo rikobuga, erinde riasaa ang'e n'ase risegesete omote.
(A beetle. It makes a sound when gnawing wood, then diarrhoeas.)

5. *Esasati.*
(Elephant grass.)

6. Amabere are enyari ime.
(Milk in the udder.)

7. Embeera.
(A grave.)

8. Chikong'a ibere chigotuma.
(Two crested cranes jumping up and down).

M

1. *Esindani esire, nabo naende okogora ey'ebwate engoro eyemo buna eyio.*
(A needle: when it is lost you buy another one also with one hole).

2. *Ekegwesi gekonyugwa.*
(A smoking pipe in use.)

3. *Ebirore*
(Spectacles.)

4. *Etaya ekobekwa amaguta.*
(A lamp/lantern, when it is being fuelled.)

5. *Amatimbo agoturungania ebiborongose bi'esike.*
(Beetles carrying dry balls of dung.)

6. *Ekegwesi kegoteebia omonwa.*
(The smoking pipe telling the mouth.)

N

1. *Embura ekogusa buna omonto ogokong'onta amao gakoyaanora.*
(The wind before the rain starts to fall. It sounds like hides being put together.)

2. *Enyongore ko yakunirwe nigo ekweringania yakira kiri.*
(Millipede. When touched, it coils up and stays still.)

3. *Omosunte obotuko.*
(A dark night.)

4. *Etinga y'amache, orogena rokona goetanana.*
(The watermill, with its grinding stone going round.)

5. *Ebaraara ekobuga.*
(An ibis making noise.)

6. *Egetenyanko.*
(A pupa of an insect in its cocoon made of small sticks.)

7. *Rikorominyo.*
(A snail.)

8. *Ritusia.*
(Big tick)

9. *Enyoni n'omoengwe.*
(A bird and a piece of wood or stick hurled at it.)

10. *Enswe erusigwe amache ime na gotigwa ase aomo egeka, goika ekwe.*
(A fish; if taken out of water for long, it dies.)

11. *Ekebabe giakinire, nakio ng'ina omwororo. Ekebabe gekomera bono, kere ekioge gekobeta, nakio abana abatindi.*
(Thatch grass. When young it is sharp and it pricks, but when mature it is soft.)

12. *Enkoba ko yaakire, nigo ekogosa abanto korende onde tamanyeti buna ere.*
(Thunder and lightning. It frightens, yet no one knows its features.)

O

1. Engoko ko yabiarire rigena, nabo ekobuga.
(The hen makes that kind of sound when it has laid an egg.)

2. Risosa nigo rire n'amato amange, korende emiongo nse ekobera.
(The pumbkin has many leaves yet its fruits lie on the bare ground.)

3. Eriko
(The three-stone hearth)

4. Esanduku y'egetondo.
(Coffin.)

R

1. Amamiria agoichora chimioro ime, erine amanya gosiomeria/komonia).
(Mucus that fill the nostrils, then peeps out of them.)

T

1. Enkoba koyaakire abanto nigo bagokira kiri.
(Thunder. Everyone keeps quiet when it roars.)

2. Enyama ekogoberera obokima ekero ogoetaneria.
(Ugali on its way down the throat, leaving the meat behind among the teeth.)

3. Enkene.
(Tape worm.)

Section Three

A

1. Ise oramoire.
(The father is the one who can take her.)

2. Omokungu ore morito naende oberegete omwana.
(A pregnant woman carrying a baby.)

3. Kare nigo yagateebekanire ng'a orute egekondo omoengwe, nakerokio nigo kegotwa oyoye gekorute. Onye aya n'amaene, rirorio nigo orabombe amaroba buna ritunda, erinde orute egekondo ekio. Gekorora igo, getwe ritunda gekorute gocha engegu. Erinde orimokie orie.
(You will throw a lump of soil at the monkey up on the fruit tree and it will throw you a fruit in turn.)

4. Esese n'ekemoni nabio amanyanyimbo atugire. Esese yaseria abaibi botuko; ekemoni giaseria chimbeba korwa nyomba.
(Dog and cat. The dog guards the home from thieves at night, while the cat chases away rats during the day.)

B

1. Osiikire, nakwo otindekire. Ekenoko ekebese, nakio omera. Abagere nigo banchete korokana Omera. Barabwo kare tibare kwaroka. Ekenoko nigo kenga riko rirabu rigotooka ase emebere y'abanto batarogeti. Nakio kiagerete ekenoko gekarokwa Omera.
(To "plant" refers to the mixing of flour and water in a

plastic paper and burying it in the ground to ferment. "*Omera*" refers to the people who do not get circumcised and hold white stuff in their penis that resembles the fermented flour.)

E

1. Ekemoni kiarinire emesa igoro keganyete embeba.
(A cat on the table waiting to catch a rat.)

K

1. Orogena narwo eng'ombe. Ensio nero emori.
(The base grindstone is the cow and hand-held grindstome is the calf.)

2. Omwana k'aiboirwe nigo akwagurera amaru abere n'amaboko abere. Ogokina otaarera amagoro abere. Okogota otaarera amagoro abere n' enyimbo.
(When born a child crawls on two hands and two legs. When he grows up he walks on two legs. When old he uses a walking stick, which represents a third leg.)

3. Egetanyagora nchera. Geise gotamboka enchera nigo kegokwera aroro. Nabo bagoteeba.
(Type of rodent that excretes a certain liquid that cements pieces of wood round it. This rodent never crosses a road; it is believed if it does it will die.)

4. Ritoke nigo rikwama engote eyemo yoka, riagechwa, erinde riagunda.
(A banana plank. It gives one bunch of banana, and then dies.)

5. Oromeme rokona konyegera monwa ekero omonto ogokwana.

(Tongue. It moves inside the mouth when a person speaks, and only peeps out once in a while.)

6. *Omorero noro omogaka ore nyomba. Erioki nario chimbuche chikare gotara isiko.*
(The fire is the old man in the house and its smoke is grey hair that sprawls out.)

7. *Ekebando kegosimekwa, kiama kere n'amasakara.*
(A maize seed: it is naked when planted, but dressed up with leaves when harvested.

8. *Echiro nero omote. Egoichora mambia, nakwo ogosicha mambia. Abanto bagocha echiro nabwo ebisicha.*
(This refers to the market. It nomally fills up in the morning. It becomes empty in the evening.)

9. *Ensa geichire amachira, nario ekobuga. K' ayeereire, nigo egokira kiri.*
(This refers to a clock/watch. It ticks or chimes when it has been wound.)

10. *Emonyo.*
(Ant.)

11. *Entamame.*
(Chrysanthemum.)

12. *Omonyoncho.*
(A big round basket with a small mouth used among the Abagusii community to store food, especially grains and legumes.)

13. *Ebirengererio bikare are.*
(Distant thoughts.)

14. *Amaiso: nabo akorora kende gionsi kere nonye ng'umbu eria.*
(Eyes. They can see things even on the other side of the river.)

15. *Engoro y'eguto.*
(The anti-bear's hole.)

16. *Rimore ri'omorogi rikomesa.*
(A witch's banner shining at night.)

17. *Engi.*
(Fly.)

18. *Ritang'ani nyambokie embori. Eria kabere nyambokie enyang'au, nyetigeo yoka, ng'iranie embori gocha aiga. Eri a'gatato nyambokie ebara, inyetige n'enyang'au. Eri a kane nyambokie embori.*
(First I will carry the goat with me. Next I fetch the hyena. I will leave the hyena on the other side of the river and come back with the goat. Leave the goat here alone and take with me the limesalt. I will leave the limesalt with the hyena and then come back to fetch the goat.)

M

1. *Amaiso arora egechure. Amagoro akeminyokia. Amaboko ageita. Omonwa okeria.*
(The eyes saw the antelope. The legs chased it. The hands killed it. The mouth ate it.)

N

1. *Enda. Enchara ko yakonyarire nigo okogora endagera rigori riaye nariba igoro.*
(Stomach. Once hungry, you will buy food at the market price for any price.)

2. *Ebibiriti, nonya n'ebite biabo nigo bigwekaine.*
(Match boxes and match sticks; both look alike in any shop you buy them from.)

3. *Obotigatigi. Nabwetigatigia togoseka.*
(Tickling. You cannot laugh if you tickle yourself.)

4. *Omotembe osichete ebisicha ebibariri.*
(*Omotembe* tree with red flowers on it.)

5. *Ekiara egeke giokoboko gwokobee.*
(The small finger of the left hand.)

O

1. *Chimioro onye chiroria igoro, ekero okwemiria, tanga amamiria nigo agotwa buna embura.*
(Nostrils. If they faced up, mucus could fall like rain when you blow your nose, and could kill many people.)

2. *Endege egoeta igoro, nero omwana. Endumo yaye ekoigwekana nyuma nero ebirero.*
(The aeroplane is the child; its sound, which is heard far behind it, is the funeral.)

www.ingramcontent.com/pod-product-compliance
Lightning Source LLC
Chambersburg PA
CBHW030054170426
43197CB00010B/1526